YOU CAN BE A BUSINESS PERSON TOO!

A Kid's Guide to the World of Business

Dr. Anthony Clark, PhD

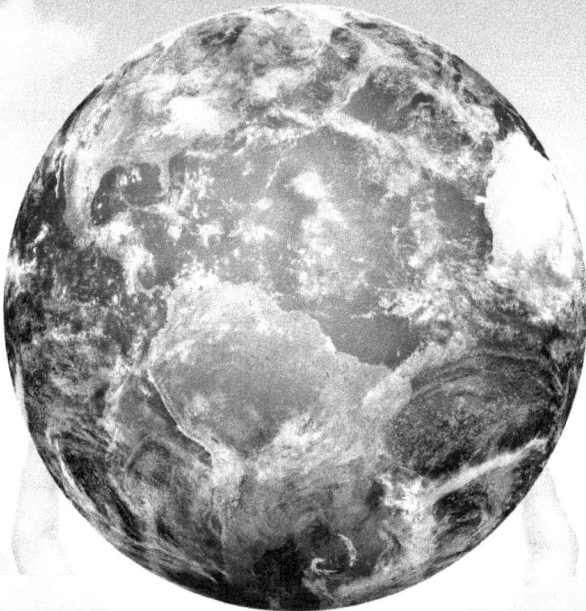

This book may be ordered through booksellers or by contacting:

iGlobal Educational Services, LLC
PO Box 94224
Phoenix, AZ 85070
www.iglobaleducation.com
512-761-5898

Because of the dynamic nature of the Internet, any web addresses or links contained in this book may have changed since publication and may no longer be valid. The views expressed in this work are solely those of the author and do not necessarily reflect the views of the publisher, and the publisher hereby disclaims any responsibility for them.

This is a work of fiction. Names, characters, businesses, places, events, and incidents are either the products of the author's imagination or used in a fictitious manner. Any resemblance to actual persons, living or dead, or actual events is purely coincidental.

You Can Be a Business Person Too! A Kid's Guide to the World of Business

ISBN-13: 978-1-944346-63-8

$$
DEDICATION

To Brendan, Abed, and Mamoun...three young entrepreneurs who are doing great things in the world.

$$

CHAPTER 1
Business Is All Around You

You probably know what business is, or at least you can make a pretty good guess about it. When people trade goods and services for money, they're doing business. A business is also a company that sells goods and services.

A store like Toys-R-Us is a business. A restaurant like McDonalds is a business. A teenager in your town who gets paid to walk dogs also has a business. A business can have one worker, or it can have thousands. A business with only a few workers is called a small business.

Goods and Services

Goods are things like clothes, cars, bicycles, and hula hoops. If you buy an object you can hold or look at or play with, then it's a good. It's also a good if you can eat or drink it. A chocolate shake is a good. So is a pair of shoes.

Services are different than goods because there's nothing to hold or look at. You've most likely gotten haircuts. A haircut is a service (sure, you can see a haircut after it's finished, but you can't hold a haircut or store it or resell it). Merry Maids is a well-known company that cleans its customers' houses. House cleaning is a service. Internet service is . . . . you guessed it: a service.

Some businesses only sell goods. A restaurant like Dunkin Donuts only sells goods like donuts, coffee, and other food items. Other businesses only sell services. A taxi tab company offers rides to its customers, and that's a service. A taxi cab company doesn't sell goods to its riders. But there are a lot of companies that sell both goods and services. A car dealer is a good example. People go to a car dealer when they want to buy a new car. Many car dealers, in addition to selling cars, offer car repair services. Many hair stylists also sell hair care products, like shampoo and conditioner.

Think about the money you spend each week or each month—your own money and your parents' money. Do you mostly spend money on goods or on services? What kinds of goods do you buy? Do you pay for any services, like haircuts or grooming for your pets?

The people who work in business are known as *businesspeople*. Sometimes women who work in business are called *businesswomen*, and men who work in business are *businessmen*. A man or a woman can be a *businessperson*.

You've probably already done a lot of business in your life. If you've gone into a grocery store and bought a pack of gum, you've done business. If you've purchased a toy or video game, you've done business. In those kinds of situations you were doing business as a customer or consumer. If you start your own business—like a dog walking business—then you'll be doing business a different way. You'll be doing business as a businessperson.

A person who starts his or her own business is a business owner. There's another special term for a business owner. A business owner is also known as an *entrepreneur*.

You don't have to be an entrepreneur, or business owner, to work in business. There are lots of jobs, many different roles, for people who want to work as businesspeople. This book outlines the basic roles people play in businesses. You'll learn about people who market and sell goods and services. You'll also learn about people who work with money, people who work with technology, and people who buy things for a living. In the next chapter you'll learn about the people at the top: the ones who manage small and large businesses.

Try This Activity

Use the Internet, or ask a knowledgeable person in your area, to help you identify the biggest business in your town. It may be obvious which one is the biggest, but you may be surprised by what you learn. Also try to find a very small business in your town. See if you can find out how many people work at the small business and how many people work at the biggest business. You'll probably discover that the big business has a *whole* lot more workers than the small businesses. Even though a big business has a lot more workers than a typical small business, there are a lot more small businesses in America than big ones. So don't let the label fool you—small businesses are *very* important businesses.

$$

CHAPTER 2
You Can Be a Manager

Do you have what it takes to be a good manager? There are several qualities a manager must possess in order to be successful. Managers need to be good communicators. They need to be able to adapt to change. They should be well-organized. They also need to be motivated, honest, and dependable. Perhaps most importantly a good manager must work well with people.

You may not know if you have all of these qualities or not. You know you're honest—or *hopefully* you know that about yourself. You likely know whether or not you work well with others, and how your communication skills stack up compared to other kids your age. People, like your parents or teachers, have probably told you things about yourself that can help you decide how motivated and dependable you are. Part of being motivated includes having the willingness to take initiative. Are you someone who gets things started without anyone else having to ask you to do so? Do you gather your friends together for a softball game or a game of tag afterschool? That's initiative. Do you think of ways to raise money for the local animal shelter, or some other cause you're passionate about? That's another example of initiative. If you're someone who likes to get the ball rolling, then you're probably a pretty motivated person.

What is a Supervisor?

"Supervisor" is another word for manager. In some companies, *Supervisor* is an actual job title, or part of a job title (e.g., Production Supervisor, Second-shift Supervisor, etc.). In a more generic sense, a supervisor is someone who is in charge of other workers in a company. A worker's supervisor is the person he reports to directly.

A characteristic that's necessary for the top leader of an organization is *vision*. A leader with vision easily comes up with new ideas for the company, and can chart new courses for the company. The late Steve Jobs, co-founder of Apple, is a good example of a visionary leader. He could imagine people using new computer devices, like the iPad and the iPhone, long before the devices were even created. Vision is a great quality for any manager to possess, but it would be hard for a top manager to be effective without it.

The top manager of a company is sometimes the president of the company, or sometimes she's called the CEO, which stands up for *chief executive officer*. It takes a lot of talent and drive to become a CEO. Because a CEO has a lot of responsibility on her shoulders, the job can be very stressful. It can also be a very rewarding job for a person who thrives on new challenges. However, most people who work in business are not CEOs or top managers. A large business usually has lots of managers, along with many other workers who aren't managers but who would still be considered businesspeople.

Different companies have different names, or titles, for their managers who work under the president or CEO. Some have titles like Vice President, Director, District Manager, or Regional Manager. Some have titles related to the specific area they manage—e.g., Manager of Operations.

So Many Chiefs

In addition to having a CEO, many large companies also employ other high-level managers with the title of "chief." They include CFO (chief financial officer), COO (chief operating officer), and CIO (chief information officer) or CTO (chief technology officer). Some companies have even more chiefs, such as the CCO (chief compliance officer), CSO (chief security officer), and the CMO (chief marketing officer).

There are also department managers, store managers, and assistant managers. There's no end to the kinds of managers a company can employ. There's also no end to the titles you can find for managers in business organizations.

Super Creative Manager Titles

Bidlack, a creative agency, refers to its accounting manager as the *Director of Bean-Counting*, and a company called

Delivering Happiness employs a *Money Maestro*. Eyespeak, a website development company, has a *Director of Storytelling*, and another company, Opportunity Network, calls its Human Resources Manager the *Chief People Officer*. Quicken Loans has a position most other companies don't (but most could probably use): *Vice President of Miscellaneous Stuff*. Quicken's *VP of Miscellaneous Stuff* is responsible for . . . miscellaneous stuff, of course. Shepard Presentations has what is perhaps the most creative title for a manager. The title belongs to the company's founder, who refers to himself as the company's *Chief Amazement Officer*.

Managers You'll Find in Most Companies

Although the titles may differ from one company to another, most large and medium-sized companies employ an operations manager, a human resources manager, an IT manager, an office manager, a marketing manager, a sales manager, and an accounting manager, often known as a controller.

An **operations manager** supervises the production of a company's goods and services. The operations manager makes sure the company's production processes, or operations, run smoothly and efficiently. The operations manager is usually in charge of quality control, or of making sure the company's products aren't broken or defective. A person in this role will likely handle a lot of hiring, and will also need to make sure the company's operations stay within budget.

What Does It Mean to Be Efficient?

"Efficient" may be a word you've heard adults use before. It's an important word, and a very important concept in business. When a company is being efficient it means that the company is producing its goods and services in the least costly way possible, without being wasteful. That doesn't mean that the company is producing cheap junk. The company may be producing expensive goods, like diamond rings or yachts, but it's still producing those luxury items at the lowest possible cost. An individual can also be efficient. If you walk to your friend's house using the shortest route possible, then you're being efficient because you're not wasting time. If you've figured out a faster way to rake the leaves in your front yard, then you're being efficient. Companies that aren't efficient usually end up losing money, or they may even end up going out of business in the long run.

A **human resources manager** may not make most of the hiring decisions a the company, but the HR manager will advertise for potential workers, set up the interviews, and handle all the paperwork when the company makes new hires. Many HR managers set up training programs for a company's workers. They interview workers who are leaving the company, and they handle the paperwork when workers are fired. HR managers also oversee a company's benefits programs, such as health insurance, savings plans, and gym memberships.

A company's **IT manager** is the person in charge of a company's computers and information systems. "IT" stands for information technology. The IT manager makes sure a company's workers have the computer hardware and software they need. IT managers may not make repairs themselves, but they make sure the computers get fixed when something goes wrong. They also update the company's software whenever it's needed.

The duties of an **office manager** can vary a lot from one company to the next, but most of them supervise the company's secretarial and support staff. They make sure the office and the company's basic administrative services run smoothly.

A **marketing manager** is in charge of promoting a company's goods and services. The marketing manager will decide what kind of advertising the company will do. The marketing manager will usually also send out press releases to let the media know when the company has new products.

A **sales manager's** duties are different from those of a marketing manager. A sales manager supervises the company's team of salespeople. It's the sales manager's job to make sure the salespeople meet their sales goals.

It seems like the company's **controller** would control everything in the company, but that's not the case. The controller, or accounting manager, oversees the company's accounting department. The controller makes sure certain reports, called financial statements, are completed on time. The controller makes sure company's accounts are balanced and that the company's taxes get paid each year.

Try This Activity

Find someone in your family, or maybe a family friend, who works as a manager in a small or large company. Ask that person to tell you about her job. How long has she been doing the job? What did she do before she became a manager? What kind of education or training did she pursue before landing her job? How does she like her job as a manager? What's the best part of her job? What's the most challenging part of her job? What would she like to change about her job, if anything? What other kind of manager jobs exist within her company? Does your family member or friend plan to climb higher in her company or another organization? Would she like to be a top manager—the president or CEO of a company—one day?

A smaller company may only have one person overseeing each department, or each area, of the company. But a large company will likely have lots of managers. If you drew a picture of how the managers are organized in a large company, it might look something like a layer cake. You would see more managers on the bottom layer, fewer managers in the middle layers, and very few managers at the top. The managers on the bottom layer report to the managers on the next layer up. At the top of the cake are the upper-level managers, the CEO, COO, CFO, and so on.

As mentioned earlier, a manager's job can be stressful, especially for high-level mangers. But it can also be an interesting and rewarding career. Managers often make important decisions that impact a lot of people. The best managers inspire and uplift the people who work for them, and that's a very rewarding way to spend the workday. If you believe you possess most or all the qualities good managers need, then you might consider becoming a manager one day.

Who knows? If you work hard and you're motivated enough, you may even become the *Chief Amazement Officer* for a company you create in the future.

$$

CHAPTER 3

You Can Be a Salesperson

Salespeople sometimes get a bad rep. It's easy to stereotype salespeople as pushy, dishonest, and greedy. A few bad salespeople, working in a wide range of industries, have created a negative stereotype that affects everyone working in sales. The truth is that sales is an important profession, and it's an honorable one. Good salespeople help customers learn about products and choose the ones that will best satisfy the customers. A good salesman or saleswoman doesn't plot against the customer. A real sales professional is in the customer's corner, working with the customer to achieve a good outcome for everyone.

Hard Selling Versus Soft Selling

A hard sell is sale that comes about because the salesperson pressures the customer to buy the product. A soft sell involves the salesperson educating the customer about the product and letting the consumer come to understand and appreciate the benefits of the product. Many people are put off by hard selling tactics. Some people are even offended by such tactics. Those people think of hard-selling salespeople as annoying and dishonest. A soft sell takes more time, and so the salesperson must be more patient. To make a soft sell, a salesperson needs to be a good listener. She also needs to genuinely care about helping the customers solve their problems. It's probably obvious that most customers greatly prefer soft selling techniques.

What Makes a Good Salesperson?

Good salespeople share many of the same qualities as good managers. They need to be smart and motivated. They also need to have good people skills. In particular, the best salespeople tend to be extroverts. They enjoy meeting new people and making new friends, and they're good at both. They thrive in social situations. A true extrovert would rather spend time with others than spend time alone. If you're an introvert, you could still be a good salesperson, but you'll have to work harder to pull off what comes naturally for the extrovert. Along those same lines, good salespeople are usually charismatic. That's a big word that essentially means people like you. Maybe you've met someone who is likable for no other reason than she happens to be likable. That's charisma—a person who has charisma is charismatic. A person like that could possibly be a good salesperson one day.

In addition to being likable, good salespeople are upbeat and confident. They know they won't close every sale, but they know they'll close enough of them. When a sale is made—when the customer decides she wants the product—people say that the sale has been *closed*.

Who Are You Selling To?

It's important for a salesperson to know who his target customer is—or, in other words, what type of customer would benefit most from the product. Some salespeople sell their products directly to households or individuals. There's an interesting abbreviation for sales made directly to consumers. They're called "B2C" sales, which stands for business-to-consumer. For example, a company that sells shutters to homeowners is involved in B2C sales. Other salespeople sell to businesses, and such sales are sometimes referred to as "B2B" or business-to-business sales. A salesperson who sells cleaning services to homeowners and to businesses would be engaged in B2C and B2B sales.

It's important for a salesperson to be confident because every sales professional faces rejection. Every salesperson will hear *no* more than he hears *yes*. That's just how it goes in the world of sales. A confident salesperson knows he'll get to a *yes*, and he'll be rewarded when that happens. As he gains more skill, a good salesperson learns how to convert more of the *nos* and *maybes* to *yesses*.

Inside and Outside Sales

Sometimes you hear businesspeople talking about inside sales and/or outside sales. Inside sales is usually done in an office, although some inside salespeople work from home. An inside salesperson reaches customers over the phone or using the Internet. An outside salesperson goes out to meet potential customers in person. Years ago, people talked about "door-to-door" salespeople. These men and women went and knocked on the doors of people's houses, trying to sell them vacuum cleaners, cleaning supplies, food items, and any number of other goods and services. There are still door-to-door salespeople working today, but not as many as there were in years past. Most outside salespeople visit businesses because that's who their customers are.

The Sales Process

If you did a search you could find thousands of books and articles offering sales strategies, tips, and tricks. There are many different ways to think of the sales process, but it boils down to a few basic steps: prospecting for leads, approaching the prospect, making the sales presentation, handling objections, closing the sale, and customer follow up.

Prospecting for Leads

If you were trying to sell dollhouses, you wouldn't approach every person on the street about buying one. For example, if you saw a family that included two little girls, that would be a good family to approach about buying one of your dollhouses. A fifty-year-old man who has no children or grandchildren might want a dollhouse, but most likely not. You would waste a lot of time approaching fifty-year-old single men about buying dollhouses. It would be a much better use of your time to find parents or grandparents of girls. When you work to identify the people who would most likely need or want your product, you're prospecting for leads.

Approaching the Prospect

You could approach the prospect face-to-face in person or over the phone. Actually you could also approach a prospect through email or snail mail, but most salespeople expect to talk to their prospect on the phone or in person. You'll want to prepare yourself so you know the best way to approach your prospect. You might start off by asking a question. Or you might offer a small gift to the prospect. If you don't have a way to get the prospect's attention and interest right off the bat, then the sales process will be over quickly.

Making the Sales Presentation

Once you've gotten your prospect's attention, you can proceed with your sales presentation. Most salespeople practice their presentations. They don't want to fumble and stutter while talking about their products. At the same time, you don't want your sales presentation to sound too "canned," or too much like a voicemail recording. In your sales presentation, you'll point out the features and benefits of your product. A good sales presentation is designed to help the prospect become more interested in your product, so interested that he or she is moved to want to buy your product.

Features and Benefits

In their sales presentations most salespeople highlight the features and benefits of their products. The features are often easy to see, but the benefits may have to be pointed out to the prospect. A feature is a characteristic of the product, a basic fact about it. Benefits are what the product actually does for a customer. Consider a specially designed pillow that has a curve built into it—or, in other words, it's not a typical flat pillow. The curve would be a feature of the pillow. A benefit would be that it helps a person sleep more comfortably.

Handling Objections

At some point during your sales presentation, your prospect will likely have an objection—a reason she can't or won't buy your product. The prospect may say that the product is the wrong color, or that it costs too much, or that another company has a better version of the product. It's the salesperson's job to handle objections like these so that they don't keep the prospect from buying. For example, if you were selling cars and your prospect said the car you're demonstrating is the wrong color, you might overcome that objection by pointing out that the same model is available in many colors. If the prospect said she didn't have enough money to buy a particular car, you might offer her a payment plan. If she said she's considering another model of car (which is sold by a competitor down the street), you'll want to point out why your product—the car you're offering for sale—is a superior vehicle. If the prospect has any objection the salesperson can't overcome, then the sales process may be derailed.

Closing the Sale

Closing a sale is part science and part art. Some salespeople are naturally good at it. New salespeople are often afraid to ask for the sale, but that's what you have to do as a sales professional. If your sales presentation is designed well, and you do a good job overcoming your prospect's objections, then it shouldn't be too difficult to ask for the sale. How do you know if the sale is closed or not? When the prospect pays for the product or signs a contract, the sale is closed. The prospect has officially become a customer!

Follow Up

In many industries, the salesperson's job isn't finished when the sale is closed. A good salesperson will follow up with the customer to make sure the product is meeting the customer's needs. One reason to follow up with customers is so that they don't return the product. If a customer returns a product, it's the same as if the sale has been cancelled. Also, if you follow up with a customer and make sure she's happy she'll more likely tell her friends about your product. It's much easier to sell to someone who has been sent to you—or referred—by another satisfied customer. And, of course, following up with a customer will increase the odds that she'll come back to you the next time she needs to purchase your product.

Try This Activity

Pick something you no longer need or want, like a toy or a book, and try to sell it to someone. Make sure it's in good shape, and that it's something another person would actually want (not a broken toy or a book that has its pages ripped). Think about which of your relatives or friends might most benefit by owning that particular object. Put together a sales pitch. What are the features and benefits of the object—your product? What can you say about it to make it appealing to your potential customer? Only tell the truth about your product. You want to point out its features and benefits without lying or exaggerating. Remember not to hard sell your customer. There's no need to be pushy or aggressive. Also, don't get angry or offended if the person doesn't want to buy your product. Remember that you may have to hear several *no*s before you get to a *yes*. (If people keep telling you *no*, it's also possible that you've set your price too high.) Notice whether you enjoy the sales process or not. How well did you do at selling? Were you able to sell the object—your product—at a fair price? Based on what you learned, do you believe you have what it takes to become a truly excellent salesperson?

$$

CHAPTER 4
You Can Be a Buyer

Are you one of those people who loves to go shopping? Did you know there are people who get paid to shop? That may sound hard to believe, but it's true. There are people who have job titles such as Buyer, Purchaser, and Purchasing Agent. They don't get paid to buy things for themselves—sorry if that's the idea you got. Buyers, Purchasers, Purchasing Agents, and others with similar job titles get paid to buy goods for the companies that employ them.

You might think it seems strange that a company would *buy* things. Aren't companies supposed to sell goods and services to customers? Of course, that's what companies do to earn a profit. But they have to first buy the merchandise, or the goods, they're going to resell to their customers. Actually, there's a little more to it than that. Retail stores, like Target and Toys-R-Us, buy merchandise and resell it. There are also wholesale companies that buy goods and resell them. For example, Baker and Taylor is a wholesale company that buys books from publishers and sells the books to bookstores.

What's the Difference Between Retail and Wholesale?

A retail sale is one that's made directly to the customer who'll be using the product. A company that makes retail sales is known as a retailer. Wal-Mart is one of the best-known retailers in the world. Amazon is another very well-known retailer. You can probably think of dozens, if not hundreds, of other retailers.

Wholesale goods go through a middleman known as a wholesaler. Many wholesalers purchase goods from manufacturers and sell them to retailers, who in turn sell the goods to the customers who use the product. Wholesalers aren't nearly as well-known as retailers. You can't just walk in and buy products off the shelf from a wholesaler. But lots of products you purchase at retail stores have gone through wholesalers before reaching the shelves. Wholesalers, it's fair to say, play just as important a role in our economy as retailers do.

Other companies buy what are known as raw goods, or raw materials, and use them to produce other goods. These companies are manufacturers. A company that manufactures automobile tires, for example, needs to buy rubber. A company that manufactures wooden rocking chairs needs to buy . . . you guessed it: wood. In these examples, rubber and wood are considered raw goods or raw materials. The tires and the rocking chairs are referred to as *finished goods*. Buyers or Purchasing Agents who work for manufacturers are responsible for making sure the company has the raw materials it needs to produce enough finished goods to sell to its customers.

Try This Activity

Find an item—a finished good—in your house. Examine the item and try to guess what raw materials were needed to produce the item. For some items, the raw goods involved will be obvious. A wooden table is made of wood. Most hammers are made of steel, or some similar hard material, and wood (for the handle). For most clothing items you can actually find out if your guess is correct by checking the tag. You can also try this activity with packaged food items, although you may only be able to guess the main ingredients such as corn, wheat, or rice. Check the label on the package to see if you guessed correctly. As you try the activity with a few different items, think of all the various raw materials the companies had to purchase in order to make the products.

What It Takes to Be a Buyer

As you might imagine, being a buyer can be a fun and rewarding job, especially if you're buying merchandise you really find interesting. Do you like clothes and fashion? Someone has to pick out the clothes, shoes, and accessories that will be sold on the shelves of department stores and other retail stores. Maybe you're into electronics and you love to read about the newest gadgets on the market. Some buyers have the job of choosing which electronics products will be made available at retail stores.

No matter what goods are being purchased, a professional buyer or purchasing agent must be a good researcher. For most goods, there are many possible vendors—many man-ufacturers or wholesalers—from which the merchandise could be purchased. The buyer has to meet a lot of vendors and sort through most or all the possible options. Sometimes buyers go and visit the plants where the goods are actually manufactured, so they can gain a more complete under-standing of the vendor and its products. A buyer needs to have basic math skills. Buying wholesale merchandise for resale and purchasing raw goods both require a bit of num-ber crunching.

A buyer should be a good decision maker, and he needs to have a good understanding of the customers' tastes. When there are so many possible options, it's important that the buyer choose the merchandise his store's customers will most want. It's also important that the buyer purchase only the amount his company needs. If he purchases too much or too little of a particular good, he'll create an inventory problem for his company. A company's inventory includes all the goods or materials it has in stock. Companies like to keep their inven-tories all small as possible—or, in other words, no larger than necessary. If inventory is too low, then the company may miss out on some sales because there's not enough merchandise to meet their customers' demand. If inventory is too large the company has to store the goods, and that costs money. Also, some types of inventory can spoil or go bad if it sits too long in storage.

In addition, a buyer needs to have good negotiating skills. A buyer has to negotiate contracts that include the price his company will pay for the goods, the quantity of goods, and the time the goods will be delivered. Some of the goods may be defective or broken when they're delivered. The contract the buyer negotiates will also spell out how defective and damaged goods will be handled.

Clearly, on top of all the other skills listed, a buyer or purchasing agent needs to have people skills. Most jobs in business involve working with people, and buyers are no different. Buyers are focused on the stuff they're buying—raw goods or finished goods—but they have to work with people to make it all happen.

Other Jobs Related to Purchasing

A professional who has experience as a buyer or purchasing agent may one day become a purchasing manager. In a large company, a buyer might only be responsible for purchasing a few different types of goods. But the purchasing manager would be responsible for all the purchases her company makes and all the contracts negotiated.

Jobs similar to the jobs of buyers, purchasing agents, and purchasing managers include supply chain analysts, supply chain managers, and logisticians.

"Supply chain" is a term that's heard in business a lot more in recent years than in the past. A company's supply chain is the whole network of vendors or suppliers it uses and any transportation or warehousing it uses. The supply chain begins with any raw goods or materials the company uses and ends with the finished goods delivered to the company's customers. If you think about it, there are some obvious similarities between what buyers and purchasing agents do and what supply chain analysts and managers do. However, for many companies, supply chain analysts and managers have bigger and broader responsibilities than buyers or purchasing managers. Supply chain analysts and managers are more involved with transportation and warehousing, and also with distributing the company's products to its customers.

A logistician is another name for a supply chain analyst or a supply chain manager. It comes from the word "logistics." Logistics was a term first used in the military and later adopted by businesses. Logistics is the management of how resources are obtained, stored, and transported.

What Is a Sustainable Supply Chain?

Companies are paying closer attention than ever to environmental issues related to their supply chains. For some managers, it's very important that their companies only purchase raw materials that are harvested in an environmentally friendly manner. For example, such managers wouldn't want to purchase materials from an endangered rainforest. They wouldn't want to buy chemicals from a company that dumps its waste into the ocean. When a company obtains its resources in a way that does no lasting harm to the environment, the company is said to have a sustainable supply chain.

Many supply chain managers and purchasing managers also consider the impact of their supply chains on human lives. These ethically minded managers don't want their companies to purchase goods from foreign firms that abuse their workers. Many managers are finding that it's good for business for their companies to develop sustainable and ethical supply chains. More than ever before, customers are asking questions about where the goods they purchase are coming from and how those goods are affecting the environment and all of mankind.

$$

CHAPTER 5
You Can Work with Money

Y ou may already be someone who likes to count and handle money. Maybe you keep close track of all the money you spend. If you're already like that, you might like to have a career one day working with money. There are several jobs that involve working with money. The process of keeping track of money in a business is known as *accounting*. Families and individuals also need to keep track of their money, and that's also a form of accounting. But much of the heavy accounting work that takes place is due to the billions of accounting transactions that occur every year in the country.

What is a CPA?

CPA stands for certified public accountant. A CPA is a business professional who has studied accounting in college and passed a special CPA exam. It takes several years of study to become a CPA. When someone calls herself a CPA, people trust that she had the necessary knowledge to handle accounting work correctly. Some certified public accountants specialize in tax work—in helping individuals and businesses plan and complete their yearly taxes. Other CPAs focus on other types of accounting work. There's always a lot accounting work that needs to be done, and so there are always jobs available for CPAs.

Profits and Losses

Accounting can be pretty complicated, and that's why accountants study their subject in college for many years. But with just a little bit of focus, you can understand some basic accounting concepts.

One key concept in accounting is *sales*. An earlier chapter discussed the sales process and careers in sales. In this chapter, sales refers to the money a business receives from selling its goods and services. Sometimes, for a business, sales is called revenue or sales revenue. Sales revenue isn't the money a business owner gets to take home. It's all the money that comes into the cash register, and into other accounts.

Another important concept in accounting is *expenses*. Your family has expenses to pay every month. Most families have to pay rent or a house payment. That's a typical expense for a family. Utilities, food, and insurance are other expenses a typical family pays on a regular basis. Expenses for a typical business include rent, utilities, and insurance, just to name a few. But businesses have expenses that most households don't. For example, most businesses pay wages or salaries to their workers. Most businesses also have an expense for marketing or advertising.

A third concept in accounting, and one of the most important concepts in all of business, is *profit*. You can calculate a company's profit using a basic formula. The formula is sales or revenue minus expenses equals profit. As an example, suppose Fred's Frozen Fish has sales for the year of $500,000 and expenses of $350,000. Fred's profit for the year would be $150,000 (which can be found by subtracting $350,000 from $500,000).

You might wonder what would happen if a company like Fred's Frozen Fish had expenses that were larger than its sales revenue. That does sometimes happen for some businesses, and it's not a good situation. Profit can indeed be a negative number. A negative profit is known as a *loss*. For instance, if Fred's sales revenue for a given year were $500,000 and the company's expenses for the year were $700,000, then Fred's would have a loss of $200,000. (If you put 500,000 − 700,000 into a calculator, you'll get negative 200,000.) A company may be able to withstand a loss in some years, but if it experiences too many losses in a row it may go out of business. Companies that are earning healthy profits don't usually go out of business.

What is Finance?

Finance is a word you may have heard, although you may not have been clear about what it means. People who work in finance often manage money or help others manage money. For example, a professional who works at a bank, setting up loans for businesses and individuals, works in finance.

A professional who helps people make decisions about buying stocks and bonds also works in finance. A large number of finance professionals work on Wall Street, where lots of stocks and bonds are traded, and many other kinds of financial transactions take place. There's a wider variety of job types in finance than in accounting. Although a person with an accounting degree can usually find a job in finance, accounting and finance are separate majors in college.

Assets and Liabilities

Other concepts you'll come across in accounting are *assets* and *liabilities*. Assets are things that are owned by a business or an individual. You probably have assets of your own. Maybe you own a bicycle. That would be one of your assets. Maybe you have your own computer. A computer is definitely an asset. Businesses typically have assets such as buildings, vehicles, equipment, computers, office furniture, and inventories.

Liabilities are amounts of money *owed* by a business or an individual. If a business borrows money from a bank, the amount the company has to pay back is a liability. If you subtract a company's liabilities from its assets, you have what's called *net worth* or *owner's equity*. Those may seem like big words, but the concept isn't hard to understand. Suppose you just bought a house and that's all you own. Suppose your house is worth $250,000, but you borrowed $150,000 from a bank to buy it. The other $100,000 that you needed to buy the house was money you had saved up in your savings account. Given these facts, your net worth would be $100,000. You would calculate this by taking the value of your asset, the house, minus the amount of money you owe on it, which would be the amount you borrowed from the bank. So $250,00 - $150,000 = $100,000.

Just like every business owner needs to know whether the business is earning a profit or a loss, every owner needs to know the net worth of his business. Some owners may have enough accounting training to do much of the accounting work on their own, but most business owners hire accountants to help them out. Large companies usually have their own accountants working in the company. Small companies typically hire an accounting firm to handle their taxes and other complex accounting work.

Try This Activity

For a week, track all of the money you have coming in and all the money you have going out. If you earn an allowance or if you get paid for doing chores, think of that money as your revenue. Think of the money you spend on toys, candy, books, video games, etcetera as your expenses. At the end of the week total up your revenues and your expenses. Did you earn a profit or experience a loss for the week? It could be an interesting to continue this activity for a month or even longer. You might be surprised by how much you spend, or by the amounts you spend on certain items. Most people—including most adults—spend more money on unimportant things than they realize. If you're trying to save up a certain amount of money, this activity can help you figure how you can cut your spending.

$$

CHAPTER 6
You Can Work with Technology

Surely you know that almost every business uses a computer, if not multiple computers. Large businesses typically employ a network of computers, along with servers and other technology necessary for the network to operate. Computers, and related technology, have made human workers more efficient, meaning that they've made it possible for workers to get more work done faster. *Lots* faster. Because they increase efficiency, computers will always play a vital role in the workplace. It takes skilled professionals to install all those computers and networks, to use them effectively, and to keep them in tip-top shape.

Computer science is the field dealing with computers and computer systems. It's also a major in college chosen by many people who wish to work with computers professionally. There are many areas of study within the broader field of computer science. Examples include database systems, programming languages, software engineering, network security, and artificial intelligence.

Can Intelligence Be Manufactured?

It may sound a little like science fiction, but scientists are working on creating what's known as *artificial intelligence*. One form of artificial intelligence involves machines, such as computers, imitating elements of human intelligence. For example, computers exist that can learn similar to the way humans do. Some computers can also solve problems. Self-driving cars use a form of artificial intelligence. It's not likely that machines will ever be able to replace the human brain, but they may be able to do more of our "thinking" than we ever imagined possible back in the early days of computers.

Computer engineering is a field related to computer science. In many colleges and universities it's a separate major—separate from computer science. Computer engineers work on designing the parts of the computer and making them work together. People who study computer engineering typically take some computer science classes, along with engineering and mathematics classes.

A third field related to computer science and computer engineering is *information technology*, which is often abbreviated *IT*. People who work in IT use computer systems to solve problems for businesses and other organizations. They design networks and databases, and they're usually required to do so within a given budget. For example, suppose Samantha's Car Rental Company needs a new system for keeping track of all the vehicles it has available for rent across the country. Samantha's IT professionals would build a system, consisting of hardware and software, to meet that specific need, along with any other business need of the company.

Some Cool Tech Jobs to Consider

The world of computers and technology changes so quickly that new jobs, and even new specialities, are being created all the time. If you think you might want to work in the technology field, but you're not sure exactly what you'd like to do, here are a few cool jobs you can consider:

Computer Programmer – All the games and apps you use on computers and smart devices were created by computer programmers. Computer programmers also develop applications for companies to help them do business more efficiently. If you like to code, or if you're good at math and logical thinking, this might be the career for you.

Mobile App Developer – Mobile app developers are basically software developers who focus on creating applications for mobile devices, like smartphones. You can begin to learn to develop mobile apps while still in school using software that makes it relatively easy.

Software Engineer – Software engineering is sort of like computer programming, but there is a difference between the two fields. Programmers may work on a small part of a larger program or application. Software engineers make sure the parts work together and that the overall application does what it's supposed to do. Software engineering is a job that will likely always be in high demand.

Data Architect – You probably know that an architect creates the plans for a house or structure. A data architect creates the plans for housing an organization's data. More companies are using data than ever before, so data architects—and other related jobs like database administrators—will be in demand for a long time to come.

Robotics Engineer/Technician – Robotics engineers are essentially mechanical engineers who also have some programming knowledge. They design, build, and test robots. Typically robots are operated and maintained by robotics technicians.

Web Developer – If you enjoy working with computers, but you also have an artistic flair, you might consider pursuing a career in website development. Every company of every size has a website, and companies are always upgrading their websites. You can study website development in college or in a specialized training program. You can also teach yourself to build elaborate websites. A lot of web developers are freelancers who work for themselves.

Geospatial Analyst – If you like working with maps—which could either be digital or paper maps—you might one day consider training to become a geospatial analyst. A geospatial analyst works with something called a *geographic information system*, or *GIS* for short. A geographic information system is a computer system that includes geographic data. Any feature that has a location in real space can appear in a GIS. Examples include roads, rivers, forests, houses, and oil wells.

Cryptographer – Cryptographers create codes to "encrypt" data or make it safe from hackers and data thieves. Some cryptographers also work on developing techniques for breaking codes. If you think that sounds like secret spy stuff, you're not far off the mark. Lots of cryptographers in the United States work for the military. But many other organizations also need encrypted data, like law enforcement agencies, banks, and credit card companies.

Most jobs in technology require critical thinking skills. That's why most people who study a computer-related field in college are required to take fairly advanced mathematics courses. If you like math and you like working with computers, you might consider studying computer science, computer engineering, or information science in college. But there are some technology careers you can enter with specialized training from a trade school, or even through self training. If you love working with computers but math is a little challenging for you, don't let that stop you from learning all you can about technology and working toward a career in the field. There's a big demand for technology workers, and most of them earn very good salaries. On top of that, technology workers get a lot of satisfaction from knowing they're doing vital work and that they're helping move business and society toward a brave new future.

CHAPTER 7
You Can Work in Business

I deally by now you understand that a wide variety of careers exist in the world of business. Some business careers are very well-known, such as sales and accounting. But there are also numerous business careers that aren't as widely known.

Business Administration is a popular major in college, and it's a valuable one. In a typical college program, students who major in Business Administration get broad exposure to business subjects. In addition to studying composition and the humanities, they take classes in economics, finance, accounting, marketing, management, and computer applications. At most colleges and universities, Business Administration students also choose a concentration area. A student takes extra classes in his or her concentration area and gains more knowledge and skills in that area. Common concentrations in Business Administration are Management, Marketing, and Finance. (Accounting is actually a whole separate major from Business Administration). Some colleges and universities offer concentrations in specialized business areas, such as Sports Management, Hotel and

Restaurant Management, Personal Finance, and Health Care Management.

What Can You Do With a Business Degree?

The Business Administration degree is the most popular degree overall in college, and the reason is that it has value in the marketplace. Some of the top jobs available to college graduates of Business programs at the bachelor's level include:

- Business analyst
- Financial analyst
- Accountant
- Account manager
- Human resources manager
- Sales manager
- Marketing manager
- Sales representative
- Administrative assistant
- Human resources generalist

It's worth noting that starting salaries for college graduates with Business Administration degrees are higher than the average starting salary for recent college graduates. However, having the degree isn't a guarantee of success. You still have to work hard, earn good grades, work on networking skills, and be the kind of professional that a manager would want to hire.

One of the best things about working in business is that you can find a way to make it relate to your own interests. For example, suppose you're interested in arts and crafts. You can begin, even as a young person, working at a store that sells arts and crafts supplies. Such a job could be an introduction to a career in business, or you could build a career with the company, working your way up into management. If one of your interests is music, you can work for a company that sells musical instruments, or an event management company that books musical acts. Every hobby and interest you can imagine has multiple related businesses that exist. And every one of those businesses needs passionate and skilled workers to make business happen.

Try This Activity

Make a short list of your hobbies and other activities you enjoy. If you play soccer on weekends or after school, put that on your list. If you read comic books and play video games, go ahead and add them to the list. Maybe you've never ridden a horse, but you enjoy reading about horses. Add horses or horseback riding to the list. Perhaps you're a reader in general—people rarely see you without a book in your hand. Put that on your list as well.

After you have a list of your hobbies and other favorite activities, go online and see if you can find at least one business related to each item you have on the list. Ideally you can find businesses located in your town or in your region, but if not, find businesses that are at least in the state in which you live. Spend some time looking through the websites of the businesses you identified. Many company websites list key personnel. Check out the job titles at each business. Chances are some of the businesses have positions you never knew existed. You may get some new ideas for possible career paths to consider.

If you want to take this activity a step further, go visit or call one of the companies you found, maybe the one related to your absolute favorite hobby or activity. Ask if you can spend a few minutes interviewing someone in the company's management. Many managers are more than willing to answer questions about their jobs and their companies. In fact, many would be flattered if you asked them an interview. In the interview, ask any question about the business that comes to mind. It's not usually considered polite to ask a person how much money he or she earns, but you can ask what a person might expect to earn starting out with the company. Ask about different positions in the company. Ask about the kind of qualities the manager looks for in a potential employee. Ask what kind of education or training a person needs to be able to work in the company. At the end of the interview ask for the manager's card, if you haven't already by that time. Hang on to it—you may end applying for a job or internship with that company one day. If you really want to impress the manager who granted you an interview, send that person a handwritten "thank you" card. When you call in the future to ask about possible job openings, that manager will likely remember you.

If you can't find any businesses related to your interests, you can always create your own business around that topic or interest one day. In fact, even if businesses do exist that are related to your hobby or interest, you can still build your own business. People who start companies are known as entrepreneurs. Some entrepreneurs are very famous, like Bill Gates, Walt Disney, Mary Kay Ash, and Henry Ford. Most entrepreneurs are people you've never heard of, but they are visionaries nonetheless. Most people in the U.S. who have jobs work for entrepreneurs, or they work for companies that were founded by visionary entrepreneurs long ago. Although most entrepreneurs aren't kids, there are plenty of kids who are entrepreneurs. The fact is, any person of any age can start and run a business. Many entrepreneurs work in business for a period of time before deciding to leave their companies to start companies of their own.

Becoming an entrepreneur is one of the many ways a young person can build a career in business. Even if you're not sure you're ready to start a business now, it's always an option you may consider in the future. The box below includes some websites and other resources you can check out if you'd like to learn more about entrepreneurship, along with some sites featuring information about careers in business general.

Resources Worth Checking Out

You Can Be An Entrepreneur Too!: A Kid's Guide to Starting a Business book by Anthony Clark (iGlobal Educational Services)

Kidpreneurs—Entrepreneurship for Kids: kidpreneurs.org

Teaching Kids Business: teachingkidsbusiness.com/entrepreneurship-program.htm

Biz Kids Educational Tools: bizkids.com/themes/entrepreneurship

Careers in Business: careers-in-business.com

Career Ideas for Business Majors—One Day, One Job: onedayonejob.com/majors/business

www.ingramcontent.com/pod-product-compliance
Lightning Source LLC
Chambersburg PA
CBHW071413200326
41520CB00014B/3416